ILLUMINATING YOUR DARK LIFE!

Birister Sharma

Dedicated to my loving wife….

Pallabi Devi Sharma

I surrendered to you, O my Lord......

"Om Namah Shivaya"

Table of Contents

One Word

Your life is full of challenges and hardships which overshadowed and engulfed your life with the darkness of unhappiness and disappointments on many occasions, but if you know how to ignite your life, then you could overpower and enlighten everything, and you could bring a bright sunshine in your life.

Your life is always on your hands. It depends upon you, how you could perceive your life; how could you live your life; what you want in your life; what you want to become in your life; what you want to do in your life; and where you want to spend your entire life. Everything depends on you. You're the master of your own life. You can do everything in your life if you devote yourself wholeheartedly.

If you want love in your life, then you can get it. If you want respect in your life, then you can get it. If you want happiness in your life, then you can attain it. If you want to achieve success in your life, then you can achieve it. If you want to win in your life, then you can make it. If you want prosperity in your life, then you can obtain it. If you want peace and contentment in your life, then you can accomplish it.

Everything is possible for you. Nothing is impossible for you if you really want to do something special in your life.

---***---

1. Love is the food of our life

Love is the food of our heart, mind and soul. Love is the breath of our life. Without love our life is death or lifeless or meaningless or worthless. We can't think or imagine anything without love.

It is only love which gives us a new meaning of our life. It is only love which teaches us the purpose of our life.

Love is the foundation of every relationship. Without love no relationships ever survive in this world.

Love is the mother of everything in this world. Love is the only medicine which heals every wound of our life. We can state that love is the herb of our life.

Without love every creature will die in this world. Love is the only source of life in this entire world. Love is the life saving energy of every creature; love is the only power which combines and binds everything in one knot of togetherness. Love brings everything under one roof or in oneness.

Love is like the air we breathe. Love is like water we drink. Love is like the fire we get warm. Love is like earth where we live. Love is like the sky, which is above us. Love is the element of our life.

Love yourself.

Love your life.

Love your world.

Love your beloved ones.

Love your friends.

Love your neighbors.

Love every creature of this world.

Love is the only way to live in this world with happiness and peace.

It is only love which will change your life.

It is only love which will change your world.

Only love can change you.

Only love can change your life.

Only love can change your world.

---***---

Think about it!

Be so busy loving your life that you have no time for hate, regret or fear.

---***---

Stop looking for the love of your life, love your life and the right person will appear.

---***---

Be in love with your life every minute of it.

---***---

Love your life because your life is what you have to give.

---***---

Life is short….So love your life…..Be happy and keep smiling.

---***---

2. Life is always full of surprises

Life is full of surprises. Life is a big mystery. Life is very unpredictable. You'll never understand it. You never know what will happen next in your life.

Sometimes your life is full of happiness and sometimes your life is full of sorrows.

Sometimes your life is full of laughter and sometimes your life is full of tears.

Sometimes your life is full of opportunities and sometimes your life is full of misfortunes.

Sometimes your life is full of comforts and sometimes your life is full of disturbances.

Sometimes your life is full of coincidences and sometimes your life is full of accidents.

This is the truth of life.

And you've to accept it willingly.

Therefore, be always prepared yourself for your life like a brave soldier.

---***---

Think about it!

Life is full of surprises. Not all these surprises are pleasant, so you need to be ready for what life brings you.

---***---

Life is full of surprises…You don't know what will hit you.

---***---

Expect the unexpected. Life is full of wonderful things just waiting to surprise you.

---***---

Life is full of surprises, but the biggest one of all is learning what it takes to handle them.

---Deborah Wiles

---***---

Life can make you smile, cry, scream, laugh, dance, jump, sing... It's just a box full of surprises, good ones and bad ones. Live it.

---***---

3. If there is life; there is also a problem

There is no life without problems. But it doesn't mean that you stop solving your problems. Every problem has its own solution. You've to find out its solution.

No matter whatsoever happens in your life, never try to run away from your problems. You never escape from the problems of your life. The more you try to run away from it the more it chases you. You can only solve your problems when you face them bravely.

Life means problems.

There is no life without problems.

The problems are the parts of your life.

Accept your problems gladly.

Face your problems bravely.

Solve your problems.

Every problem has its own solution.

But never try to run away from your problems.

The problems of your life make you strong and bold.

If you ever try to escape from the problems of your life, then you're a coward. And you've no moral right to live in this world.

---***---

Think about it!

Most of the problems in life are because of two reasons: we act without thinking or we keep thinking without acting.

---***---

Life is full of problems and solutions. The challenges that we face either destroy us or make us stronger.

---Rick Warren

---***---

Life is a journey, with problems to solve, lessons to learn, but most of all, experiences to enjoy.

---***---

Nobody has a perfect life. Everybody has their own problems. Some people just know how to deal with it in a perfect way.

---***---

If your problem in life is as big as a ship, never forget that your blessings are as wide as the ocean.

---***---

4. Never ever take tensions in your life

You're the most beautiful creation and powerful being in this world. Never waste your valuable life in unwanted stuffs so call sorrows, anxieties, stresses and tensions.

It is very common and well known dialect that *"Tension dene ka, Tension lene ka nahi." (Give tension, but don't take tension)*

Tension means having ten-sons. What will happen to a person having ten sons? Think about it.

Always remember:

Life is to live.

Life is to love.

Life is to smile.

Life is to laugh.

Life is to crack jokes.

Life is to sing.

Life is to dance.

---***---

Think about it!

Kill tension before tension kills you. Reach your goal before goal kicks you. Live life before life leaves you.

---***---

Keep the smile, leave the tension, feel the joy, forget the worry, hold the peace, leave the pain, and always be happy.

---***---

Worries and tensions are like birds, we cannot stop them from flying near us, but we can certainly stop them from making a nest in our mind.

---***---

*Don't let tensions settle in your life and
control your emotions.*

---***---

*Tension is who you think you should be.
Relaxation is who you are.*

---Chinese proverb

---***---

5. Your life is very short and special

Your life is very short and special. You never know what will happen next. Therefore, never waste your precious time. The time is ticking on and on. Try to do something great and special in your life so that you'll be remembered when you'll leave this world forever.

Don't spend your life like the lives of crawling ants and insects, and grazing animals. It doesn't matter how long you live in this world, but it does matter what, you will do in your life.

Try to leave some mark in your life. Make your every moment special and beautiful.

Your life is very short and special.

You've to do many great things in your life.

Don't waste the golden moment of your life.

Make your life meaningful.

Make your world beautiful.

Make your every moment wonderful.

Make your every day special.

Make your every week memorable.

Make your every month remarkable.

Make your every year incredible.

---***---

Think about it!

Life is too short to start your day with broken pieces of yesterday; it will definitely destroy your wonderful today and ruin your great tomorrow.

---***---

Life is short. Don't miss opportunities to spend time with the people that you love.

---Joel Osteen

---***---

Life is short, spend it with people who care and make you feel special.

---***---

Don't ever doubt yourselves or waste a second of your life. It's too short, and you're too special.

---Ariana Grande

---***---

LIFE is short. Break the RULES. FORGIVE quickly, KISS slowly, LOVE truly, LAUGH uncontrollably, and NEVER REGRET anything that made you smile.

---***---

6. You too have some responsibilities in your life

You've some responsibilities in your life. Your responsibility of life is to become a good man/woman. Your responsibility of life is to love yourself and to love your beloved ones as well as to love every living being.

Your responsibility of life is to help everybody.

Your responsibility of life is to maintain your family, and to maintain good relationships with everybody.

Try to become a responsible man/woman in your life.

Only a responsible man/woman can change his/her life and other's life.

---***---

Think about it!

Accept responsibility for your life. Know that it is you who will get you where you want to go, no one else.

---***---

You're free to do whatever you want, but you should always take responsibility for the consequences of your choices in life.

---***---

The moment you take responsibility for everything in your life is the moment you can change anything in your life.

---Hal Elrod

---***---

Life is a gift, and it offers us the privilege, opportunity, and responsibility to give something back by becoming more.

---***---

Life will bring you pain all by itself. Your responsibility is to create joy.

---Milton H. Erickson

---***---

7. Life means love

Love is the most significant part of your life. Love is the heart and soul of your life. Love yourself. If you love yourself, then only you can love everybody and everything.

Love is your life.

Love is your world.

Love your dear ones like you love yourself.

There is a great magic in love.

Love can make everything possible.

Love is your energy.

Love is your power.

Love is the driving force of your life.

If there is love, there is life, and there is a world.

If there is no love, there is no life, and there is no world.

With love you can do anything in your life. Without love you can't do anything in your life. Love can change you. Love can change your life. Love can change your world.

Love yourself.

Love your dear ones.

Love your family.

Love your neighbors.

Love your friends.

Love your work.

Love every creature of this world.

Love is the only way to live in this world with happiness and peace.

Spread the sweet fragrance of your love far and wide to make this world a better place to live.

---***---

Think about it!

Love isn't something you find. Love is something that finds you.

---Loretta Young

---***---

Time decides who you meet in your life. Your heart decides who you want in your life. Behavior decides who will stay in your life.

---***---

Love yourself first and everything else falls into line. You really have to love yourself to get anything done in this world.

---Lucille Ball

---***---

Without respect love is lost. Without caring, love is boring. Without honesty, love is unhappy. Without trust, love is unstable.

---***---

If you love life, don't waste time, for time is what life is made up of.

---Bruce Lee

---***---

8. Your life is like a big test

Your life is like a big test. Every day you're encountered with many different and difficult tests. You're surrounded with them every day. You've to face them every day. You've to prepare yourself every day. You've to fight with them every day. But you never run away from them. Even you couldn't isolate yourself from them, since you're the part of every test of your life.

Behind every test of your life there is a hidden progress, happiness and success in your life.

Life is a big test.

It'll test you about your life.

It'll test you about your world.

It'll measure your strengths and weaknesses.

It'll evaluate your energy and power.

It'll count your labor and patience.

It'll check and balance your courage and responsibility.

It'll teach you about the lessons of life.

It'll train you about the experiences of this world.

Never get terrify with the test of your life.

It'll qualify you to make you a complete man.

---***---

Think about it!

Sometimes when you wonder why you can't hear God's voice during your trials. Remember the teacher is always quiet during the test.

---***---

Life has a way of testing a person's will, either by having nothing happen at all or by having everything happen at once.

---Paulo Coelho

---***---

A gem cannot be polished without friction, nor a man perfected without trials.

---Lucius Annaeus Seneca

---***---

Every test in our life makes us bitter or better, every problem comes to make us or break us. The choice is ours whether we become victims or victorious.

---***---

Sometimes life will test you but remember this: When you walk up a mountain, your legs get stronger.

---***---

9. Try to enjoy your life

You've every right to enjoy your life. It is your birthright. Almighty God has sent you into this world not to die before your death. He has sent you to live your life in happiness and peace. Don't make yourself too busy in your materialist world that you'll forget to enjoy your life.

Make your life beautiful and meaningful. Glance around your environment, how the beautiful flowers, the colorful butterflies and the flying birds are enjoying their lives every moment.

Enjoy by yourself.

Enjoy with your beloved ones.

Enjoy with your family members.

Enjoy with your friends.

Enjoy in your work.

Enjoy your life.

Enjoy your world.

Make your life beautiful.

Make your world wonderful.

You've every right to enjoy your life.

You've every reason to enjoy your life.

---***---

Think about it!

Enjoy life today, yesterday is gone and tomorrow may never come.

---***---

Enjoy your own life without comparing it with that of another.

---***---

Don't wait for things to be perfect before you decide to start enjoying your life.

---***---

If you want to truly enjoy your life, you must be at peace with yourself.

---***---

*The trick is to enjoy life. Don't wish away
your days, waiting for better ones ahead.*

---Marjorie Pay Hinckley

---***---

10. Keep your hope alive

No matter how tough your life is; no matter how many hurdles are trying to knock you down from the paths of your life; no matter how many times you've to face failure in your life; no matter how many long days and long years you've to live your life in anxieties and loneliness, but not for a micro second never lose your hope. Always try to keep the blazing candle of your hope alive. It is only your hope which will anchor the sinking ship of your life at the seashore in the end.

If everything is turning against you;

If everything is going wrong in your life;

If everybody is walking away from you;

If everything is engulfed with the dark clouds of doubts and anxieties in your life;

Then remember one thing in your life, still you've a burning candle of hope in your life.

Always keep your hope alive, no matter whatsoever happens in your life.

It is only your hope which enlightens your dark life.

Never lose your hope.

It is only the flame of your hope which guides you whenever you wander in the dark path of your life.

No hope, no life, and no world.

Nothing will exist without hope.

If you've hope, you've life, and you've world.

Your hope is the only rays of your life.

Always keep your radiance of hope alive.

---***---

Think about it!

Never give up hope. Situations can change overnight, and problems can dissolve in the light of a new day's sun.

---***---

Hold your head high, stick your chest out. It gets dark sometimes, but morning comes. Keep hope alive.

---Jesse Jackson

---***---

If you keep hope alive, it will keep you alive.

---***---

Not dreams but night changes, not destiny
but path changes, always keep your hopes alive,
luck may or may not change, but time definitely
changes.

---Elmore Leonard

---***---

Never lose hope that your dreams will come
true because you are closer than you think.

---***---

11. Face the challenges of your life

There is nobody in this entire world whose life is only spending on the bed of roses. It is quite impossible. It is only possible in your dream world, but it is not possible in your real world. You know why, because man is born in this world to fight with the problems and the challenges of his life. His life would be meaningless and humdrum if there is no problem and no challenge in his life.

You've to face and fight with the problems and the challenges of your life, because if there is life there are problems and challenges.

There is no life without problems and challenges. The problems and the challenges are the parts of your life. However, these problems and challenges are medium to make you strong and tough, but don't make you weak and sick.

The roots of a tree become strong and tough when the wind blows very hard and furiously.

Even if your mother wouldn't face and fight with the problems and the challenges at the time your birth, you wouldn't see this world today.

If you wouldn't face and fight with the problems and the challenges at the time of your first dawdling step, you wouldn't walk and run today.

Whether you read or heard about the great life stories of the great men or women in this world, there is no one whose life is never counter with the problems and the challenges of his or her life.

They had faced and fought many problems and struggles in their lives. However, they never shed their tears, and never bowed down before any of these problems and struggles. They had accepted every struggle and every challenge of their lives with their warm hearts and fought back strongly.

Mahatma Gandhi, Abraham Lincoln, Martin Luther king, Henry Ford, Mother Teresa, and many more great men and women, they all faced and fought many countless numbers of problems and challenges in their lives.

But they never gave up. They never quit. They had conquered every problem and every challenge of their lives with brave hearts.

Eventually, they all emerged victorious, and set the remarkable marks in their lives.

Your life is full of problems.

Your life is full of challenges.

These problems and challenges are the parts of your life.

You never escape from these problems and challenges of your life.

Life is always revolved around with problems.

Life is always surrounded by challenges.

You've to face these problems and challenges with brave hearts.

You've to fight back with these problems and challenges strongly.

You're born to overcome these problems and challenges of your life.

Never afraid with these problems and challenges of your life.

Behind these problems and challenges, there are hidden triumphs in your life.

These problems and challenges of your life will not break you down and make you weak and helpless,

But these problems and challenges of your life will make you strong, responsible and independent.

These problems and challenges of your life will give you a new opportunity to change yourself and to transform yourself.

You'll never learn the art of swimming if you ever afraid of water.

If you want to become an expert swimmer, then you've to jump into the depth of water.

---***---

Think about it!

Life is full of challenges, but these challenges are only given to you because God knows your faith is strong enough to get through them.

---***---

Life's challenges are not supposed to paralyze you; they're supposed to help you discover who you are.

---***---

We don't grow when things are easy; we grow when we face challenges.

---***---

*Challenges are what make life interesting;
overcoming them is what makes life meaningful.*

---Joshua J. Marine

---***---

*Everyone faces challenges in life. It's a
matter of how you learn to overcome them and
use them to your advantage.*

---Celestine Chua

---***---

12. Happiness and sorrows are the parts of your life

Happiness and sorrows are the parts of your life like day and night.

If you'll light a lamp, then you'll always see the light along with its casting a dark shadow on the other side. What does it mean? It means, if there is light; there is shadow as well. In the same way your life is.

If there is life, there is happiness and sorrows. Both.

This is the law of this world. And you've to admit it.

If you're born in this world, then you'll get both happiness and sorrows.

You'll get both success and failure, but after facing one after another.

If you're enjoying happiness today; tomorrow you will have to face sorrow, and vice versa. But you've to prepare yourself.

Your happiness and sorrows are like day and night.

It will never last long.

Your happiness and sorrows are like seasons.

It will always change.

Accept your happiness and sorrows with your heart's content.

Happiness and sorrows are temporary.

Your life is like a bridge between happiness and sorrows.

You've to maintain both.

You've to live a balance life in both happiness and sorrows.

Never get overwhelmed when you meet the guest of your happiness that you start forgetting the host responsibility of your life.

If you're enjoying the gala nights of happiness in your bright room,

Then somewhere, in the corner most part of your room, the dark shadow of sorrow will be waiting for you eagerly.

Your happiness always teaches you to control your emotions.

Your sorrows, always teach you to keep your patience and acceptance.

Always try to maintain yourself in both happiness and sorrows.

Don't carry away with the loud noises of your happiness that you'll forget to listen to the silent approaching of your sorrows.

---***---

Think about it!

Life is strictly coded with happiness and sorrow. We can't make it work properly without one.

---***---

Happiness keeps you sweet. Trials keep you strong. Sorrow keeps you human. Failure keeps you humble. And courage keeps you going.

---***---

Strong people know how to keep their life in order. Even with tears in their eyes, they still manage to say "I'm ok" with a smile.

---***---

Sometimes sorrow, sometimes joy. But beneath it all remember the innate perfection of your life unfolding. That is the secret of unreasonable happiness.

---Dan Millman

---***---

Happiness and sorrow are inseparable….together they come and when one sits alone with you…remember that the other is asleep upon bed.

---***---

13. Accept the realities of your life

Happiness and sorrows are the parts of your life. These are the realities of your life. You've to accept both.

Success and failures are the parts of your life. These are the realities of your life. You've to accept both.

Love and hatred are the parts of your life. These are the realities of your life. You've to accept both.

Appreciations and criticisms are the parts of your life. These are the realities of your life. You've to accept both.

Respect and disrespect are the parts of your life. These are the realities of your life. You've to accept both.

Coincident and accidents are the parts of your life. These are the realities of your life. You've to accept both.

Reunion and separation are the parts of your life. These are the realities of your life. You've to accept both.

Winning and losing are the parts of your life. These are the realities of your life. You've to accept both.

Friends and foes are the parts of your life. These are the realities of your life. You've to accept both.

Creation and destruction are the parts of your life. These are the realities of your life. You've to accept both.

Birth and death are the parts of your life. These are the realities of your life. You've to accept both.

At some point of time you'll encounter with these realities of your life.

You never escape from these realities.

You've to face them all no matter whatsoever happens in your life.

You're closely connected with these realities of your life.

Even if you ever try to detach yourself from these realities of your life, you'll never get rid of it.

These realities of life are the laws of this world.

Nobody could alter these realities of life.

You, we and I, all are abided to accept these and bounded to follow in our lives.

You've to accept these realities of your life with open heart, mind and soul.

---***---

Think about it!

Don't just accept what life brings to you each day as your reality. Instead decide what you want your life to look like and then go out and make that life a reality!

---***---

When your absence doesn't alter someone's life, then accept the reality that your presence has no meanings in their life.

---***---

Open-minded people do not impose their beliefs on others. They accept all of life's perspectives and realities, doing their own thing in peace without judging anyone.

---***---

Life is not a problem to be solved, but a reality to be experienced.

---Soren Kierkegaard

---***---

The only realities in life are that you are born, and that you die. We always think we are going to live forever. The dying aspect we will never accept. The one thing about having this kind of warning is how you appreciate every single day of life.

---***---

About the author:

53

Birister Sharma is a full time author. He is also an avid reader. He loves reading, writing, and motivation. He has penned down dozens of self-help motivational books and novels so far.

You may contact him @ birister2007@gmail.com